3/10

EDGE BOOKS™

HORRIBLE THINGS

Blood-sucking, Man-Eating Monsters

by Kelly Regan Barnhill

Consultant:
David D. Gilmore
Professor of Anthropology
Stony Brook University
Stony Brook, New York

Capstone
press®

Mankato, Minnesota

Edge Books are published by Capstone Press,
151 Good Counsel Drive, P.O. Box 669, Mankato, Minnesota 56002.
www.capstonepress.com

Library of Congress Cataloging-in-Publication Data
Barnhill, Kelly Regan.
  Blood-sucking, man-eating monsters / by Kelly Regan Barnhill.
  p. cm. — (Edge books. Horrible things)
  Includes bibliographical references and index.
  Summary: "Describes a variety of popular monsters,
including real-life accounts that inspire the legends behind the
creatures"— Provided by publisher.
  ISBN-13: 978-1-4296-2292-9 (hardcover)
  ISBN-10: 1-4296-2292-X (hardcover)
  1. Monsters — Juvenile literature. I. Title. II. Series.
GR825.B284 2009
398.24'54 — dc22   2008024824

Editorial Credits
Aaron Sautter, editor; Ted Williams, designer; Jo Miller, photo researcher

Photo Credits
Alamy/Dale O'Dell, 12; Pictorial Press Ltd, 6
AP Images/Eric Gay, 15
Capstone Press/ Jonathan Mayer, 26; Karon Dubke, 4
Corbis/Sunset Boulevard, cover
Dan Carro/Mythical Monster Museum, 29
Fortean Picture Library, 13, 14, 22
fotolia/JCG, 27
Getty Images, Inc./ AFP/Tao-Chuan Yeh, 9; Imagno, 19; Keystone, 11;
    Popperfoto/Bentley Archive, 23
The Kobal Collection/Gaumont, 16; Image Ten, 20; New Line/
    Saul Zaentz/Wing Nut Films/Pierre Vinet, 25; Warner Bros, 24
Mary Evans Picture Library, 10

1 2 3 4 5 6 14 13 12 11 10 09

Table of Contents

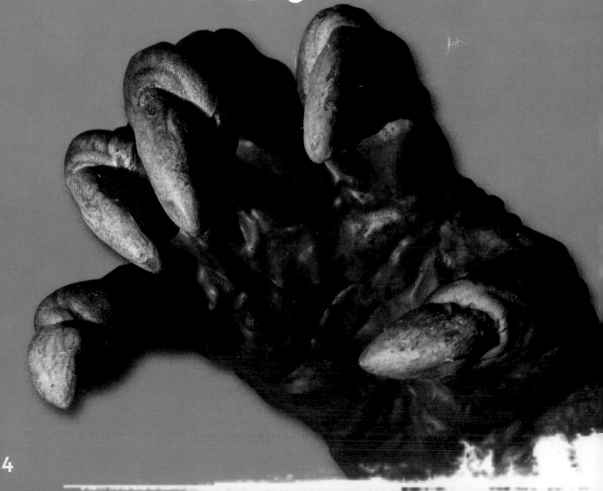

Enter if you Dare!

The hallway is long and dark. Your hands are sweaty. Your throat feels like sand. The floorboards creak as you walk toward the shadowy door. You hear the rasping breath of something waiting on the other side. What could it be? You grit your teeth and slowly turn the doorknob. Just as the door opens, a clawed hand yanks you inside!

Ugly, man-eating monsters have hidden in our scariest legends for hundreds of years. Vampires drink people's blood. Werewolves hunt during the full moon. And Bigfoot stomps through dark forests and swamps.

Where do the stories come from? Is something really prowling in the night? Or are monsters just figments of our imaginations? Are you ready to learn about the creepy things that go bump in the night? If so, grab your flashlight and turn the page — if you dare!

Werewolves

Legendary werewolves are violent, bloodthirsty creatures of the night.

On a misty, moonlit night, a fearsome creature stalks its prey. It's a monster to fear above all others — a werewolf! According to legend, werewolves normally appear as ordinary people. But when night falls and the full moon rises, they begin to change. Their noses lengthen into snouts. Their teeth grow into sharp fangs. And thick fur grows all over their bodies. After howling at the moon, they begin a tireless hunt for fresh, bloody meat.

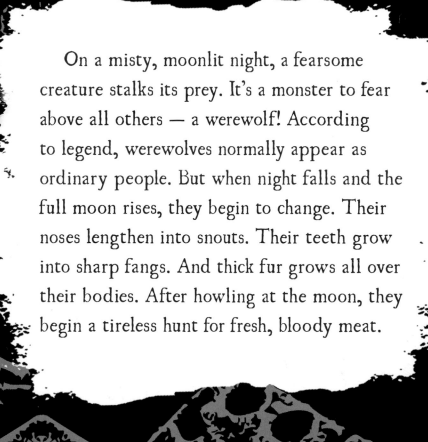

HORRIBLE FACT

Some people have a mental illness that makes them think they're turning into a wolf. These people often crawl on their hands and knees, snarl, and howl like wolves.

Werewolves are known for their large size, incredible strength, and constant hunger. Werewolves are so strong that they can carry a full-grown cow in their jaws. They run on all fours. But sometimes they stand up to use their front claws as weapons. Werewolves are ferocious hunters. They are easily tracked by the bloody trail of violence they leave behind.

There are few known defenses against werewolves. In many movies, silver bullets are the most effective way to kill a werewolf. Silver daggers are deadly to them too — if you can get close enough. When killed, werewolves return to their human form.

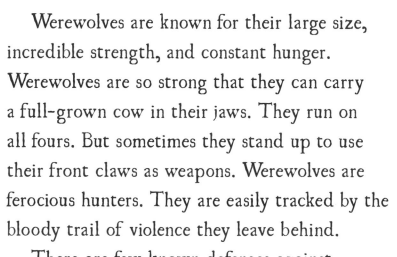

HORRIBLE FACT

In December 2007, a boy was picked up by authorities in Russia. He had no clothes. His nails were long and sharp as claws. He didn't speak, and he had no interest in people. Doctors believe he had been living with wolves since he was a baby.

REAL WEREWOLVES?

Is this man a real werewolf? Hardly. He suffers from a disease called **hypertrichosis**. The disease causes thick hair to grow all over his body. Records of people with this disease date back to the Middle Ages. It's possible that tall tales about werewolves began when people saw others with this disease.

There are still cases of the disease today. But it's extremely rare. It's only known to exist in three families in the world.

hypertrichosis — a rare disease that causes thick hair to grow all over a person's body

Giants

Most giants don't like people. They are usually unfriendly and violent toward humans.

Fee, Fie, Fo, Fum! Storytellers love using giants to spice things up. Giants are incredibly big, strong, and fierce. Their skin is thick and lumpy. They often have only one eye in the middle of their high foreheads.

Legendary giants aren't too smart. Their brains are only about the size of an egg. They usually solve their problems with clubs or fists. But not all giants are mean. Finn McCool was a clever and kind giant in Irish fairy tales. In American legends, Paul Bunyan is a hero for lumberjacks everywhere.

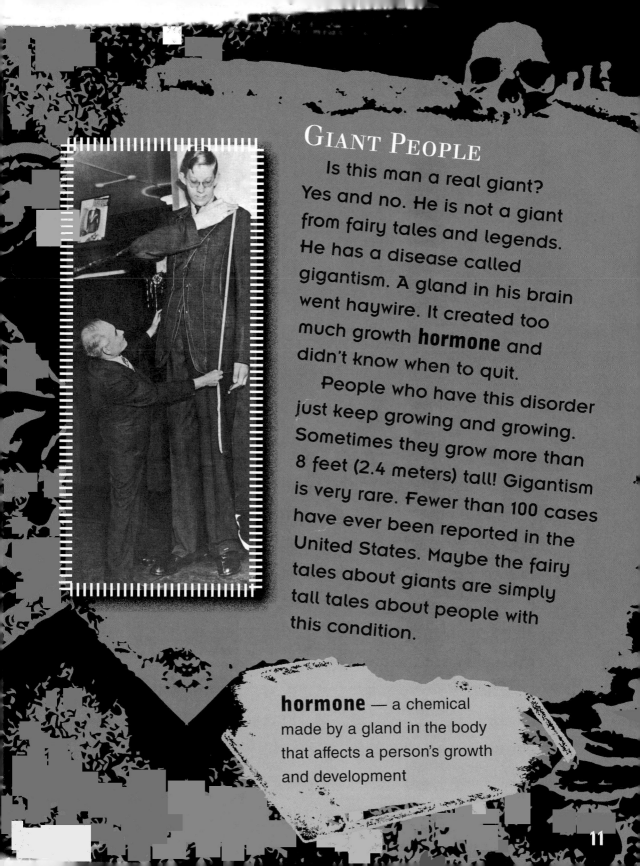

GIANT PEOPLE

Is this man a real giant? Yes and no. He is not a giant from fairy tales and legends. He has a disease called gigantism. A gland in his brain went haywire. It created too much growth **hormone** and didn't know when to quit.

People who have this disorder just keep growing and growing. Sometimes they grow more than 8 feet (2.4 meters) tall! Gigantism is very rare. Fewer than 100 cases have ever been reported in the United States. Maybe the fairy tales about giants are simply tall tales about people with this condition.

hormone — a chemical made by a gland in the body that affects a person's growth and development

Bigfoot

The creature has many names. Skunk Ape, Sasquatch, and Elder Brother are just a few. People from Washington to Florida have claimed to see Bigfoot. Most witnesses say it stands 8 to 10 feet (2.4 to 3 meters) tall. It has long arms and legs and is covered in shaggy, brown hair. And it stinks. Many people report a terrible, disgusting odor when they see the creature.

There have been hundreds of reported sightings, footprints, and hair samples. However, there is no definite proof that Bigfoot exists. No live creature has ever been captured. And no bones, dead bodies, or fossils have ever been found.

A FAMOUS ENCOUNTER

In 1967, Roger Patterson saw a big, hairy creature in the woods. He grabbed his movie camera and shot a short film of the creature. It's the most famous Bigfoot film in the world. It shows what looks like a large, shaggy creature walking upright like a person.

Most skeptics say the film is a hoax. They think it's just a man in a costume. But other people aren't so sure. A group of scientists studied how the creature moved its arms. The arms are longer than a human's, and they bend in the wrong place. The scientists believe these findings mean the creature could be a real Bigfoot.

Chupacabras

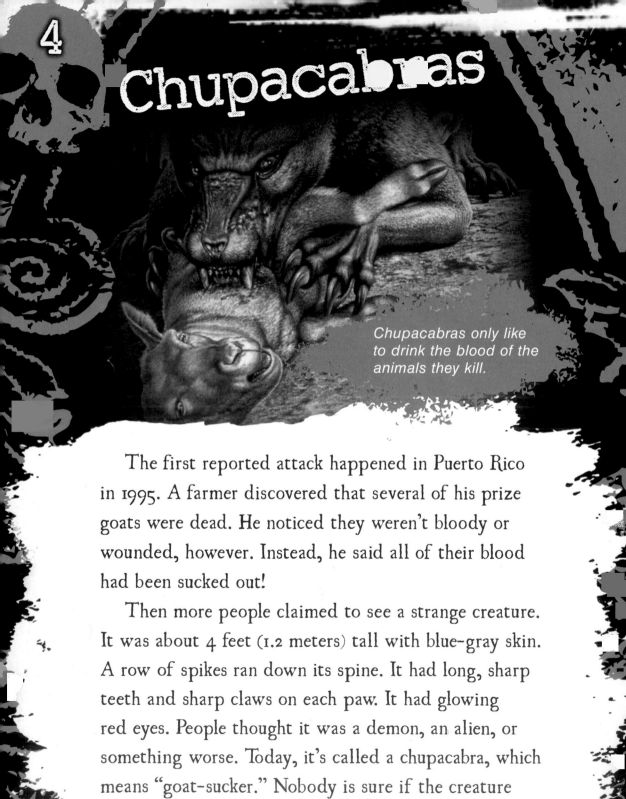

Chupacabras only like to drink the blood of the animals they kill.

The first reported attack happened in Puerto Rico in 1995. A farmer discovered that several of his prize goats were dead. He noticed they weren't bloody or wounded, however. Instead, he said all of their blood had been sucked out!

Then more people claimed to see a strange creature. It was about 4 feet (1.2 meters) tall with blue-gray skin. A row of spikes ran down its spine. It had long, sharp teeth and sharp claws on each paw. It had glowing red eyes. People thought it was a demon, an alien, or something worse. Today, it's called a chupacabra, which means "goat-sucker." Nobody is sure if the creature was imagined, or if it's still prowling in the night.

MYSTERY IN TEXAS

In 2007, Phylis Canion reported she had killed a strange animal on her Texas ranch. The animal looked like one of the mysterious chupacabras. She brought the creature to the U.S. Fish and Wildlife Service to have it tested. At first, they said it was just a sick coyote. But Canion asked for a DNA test. The tests revealed that it was a brand new animal. The creature is believed to be a mix of coyote, dog, and Mexican wolf. And there are others. Many similar sightings have been reported across the region.

07/14/2007

HORRIBLE FACT

In May 2007, a meteorite hit in the mountains of Chile in South America. Soon, many people reported seeing odd creatures with gray skin and glowing red eyes. Farmers then reported finding dead animals — with all their blood sucked out. Was the meteorite actually an alien spaceship crashing to earth? Were the creatures chupacabras? Or were they just the figments of people's imaginations? The world may never know.

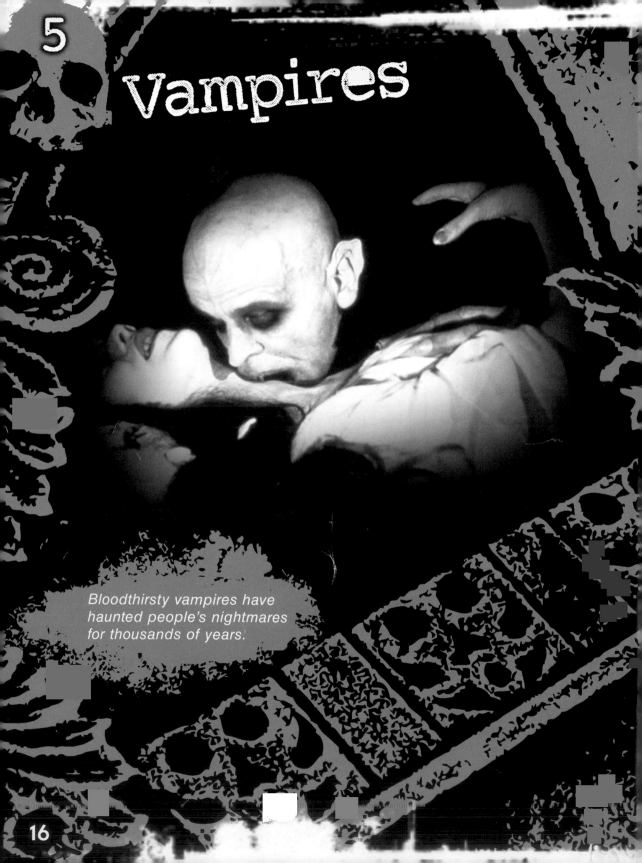

Vampires

Bloodthirsty vampires have haunted people's nightmares for thousands of years.

What's that scratching at the window? Don't let it inside! It could be a cunning, blood-sucking vampire. Tales of pale, bloodthirsty vampires have frightened people for thousands of years.

According to legend, vampires are perfect predators. They can turn into bats or other animals to sneak up on their prey. They have a keen sense of smell, sharp vision, and incredible strength. They long only for a big gulp of warm blood from their victim's throat.

In the movies, vampires are often destroyed by fire or sunlight. But the quickest way to kill a vampire is by stabbing it in the heart with a wooden stake. After that, vampire hunters make sure it's dead by cutting off the head. The safest time to kill a vampire is during the day. It's easier to sneak up on the evil creature while it sleeps in its **lair**.

lair — a place where a creature lives and sleeps

Where did people get the idea for pale, blood-craving vampires? In the Middle Ages, people worried that dead people sometimes didn't rest quietly in their graves. When strange things happened, villagers would dig up the bodies of the recent dead. If the corpse looked odd in any way, they would cut off its head and set the body on fire. They believed this was the only way to prevent the dead from walking again.

Of course, dead bodies usually did look strange. When bodies decay, the skin becomes ghostly pale, and the flesh shrinks. This causes hair, fingernails, and teeth to appear longer. It's easy to see why people thought these strange, pale corpses might rise up to attack the living.

HORRIBLE FACT

It's believed that vampires hate garlic, holy water, and crosses. People once kept these items nearby to protect themselves from the bloodthirsty monsters.

The Real Dracula

Bram Stoker's novel *Dracula* was based on a real person. During the mid-1400s, Prince Vlad Dracul III of Romania fought a bloody war against the Ottoman Empire. At the time, many people thought Dracul was a hero. He was handsome, smart, and talented. He spoke several languages, composed music, and wrote poetry.

But after several years of fierce battle, Prince Vlad became terribly violent. He started to **impale** people on large wooden spikes as a warning to his enemies. Between 1459 and 1461, Vlad ordered tens of thousands of people to be impaled. Perhaps this is how the idea of killing vampires with wooden stakes began.

impale — to thrust a sharpened stake through a person's body

Zombies

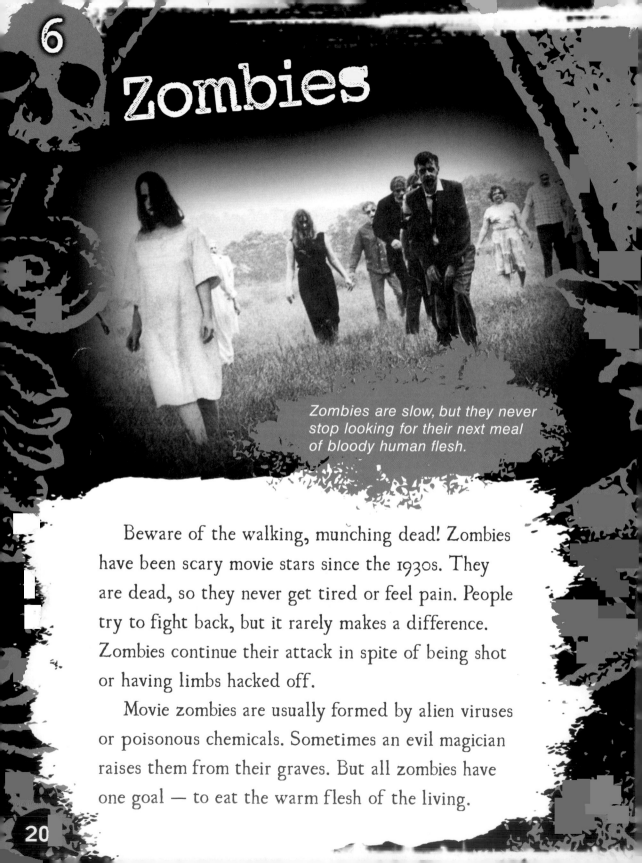

Zombies are slow, but they never stop looking for their next meal of bloody human flesh.

Beware of the walking, munching dead! Zombies have been scary movie stars since the 1930s. They are dead, so they never get tired or feel pain. People try to fight back, but it rarely makes a difference. Zombies continue their attack in spite of being shot or having limbs hacked off.

Movie zombies are usually formed by alien viruses or poisonous chemicals. Sometimes an evil magician raises them from their graves. But all zombies have one goal — to eat the warm flesh of the living.

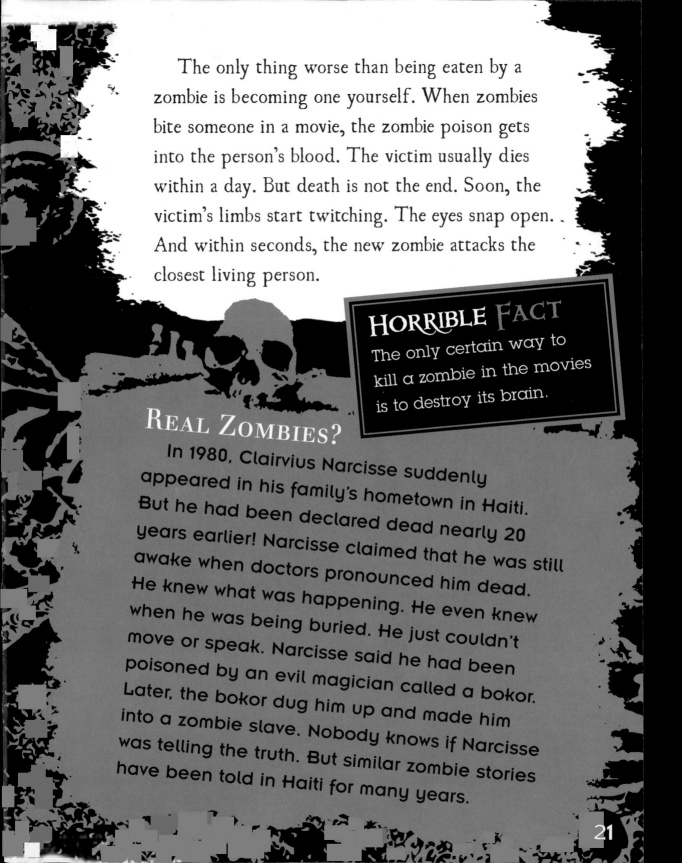

The only thing worse than being eaten by a zombie is becoming one yourself. When zombies bite someone in a movie, the zombie poison gets into the person's blood. The victim usually dies within a day. But death is not the end. Soon, the victim's limbs start twitching. The eyes snap open. And within seconds, the new zombie attacks the closest living person.

HORRIBLE FACT

The only certain way to kill a zombie in the movies is to destroy its brain.

REAL ZOMBIES?

In 1980, Clairvius Narcisse suddenly appeared in his family's hometown in Haiti. But he had been declared dead nearly 20 years earlier! Narcisse claimed that he was still awake when doctors pronounced him dead. He knew what was happening. He even knew when he was being buried. He just couldn't move or speak. Narcisse said he had been poisoned by an evil magician called a bokor. Later, the bokor dug him up and made him into a zombie slave. Nobody knows if Narcisse was telling the truth. But similar zombie stories have been told in Haiti for many years.

Sea Monsters

Deep sea fishers have found several mysterious creatures in the ocean.

In 1925, a strange, dead creature washed up in Monterey Bay, California. Its neck was about 20 feet (6 meters) long. It had large flippers and a small tail. The creature's head looked like a duck's head. Nobody knew what sort of creature it was. Was it an ancient dinosaur? Or was it something else?

The oceans are filled with mysterious creatures. People are just beginning to explore the unknown depths of the sea. Huge sharks and squids the size of school buses have already been discovered. Who knows what sorts of monstrous sea creatures might be found in the future?

SCOTLAND'S SEA MONSTER

For hundreds of years, people have claimed to see a monster swimming in Scotland's Loch Ness lake. Nicknamed "Nessie," the monster is said to have a long neck and flippers.

In 1934, Dr. Robert Kenneth Wilson took a picture of the monster. The picture showed a dark, snakelike head rising out of the water. For many years, people believed the photo proved that Nessie was real. But in 1992, the photo was revealed to be a hoax. However, that hasn't stopped people from believing.

Over the years, dozens of blurry pictures and videos have made Nessie real in the minds of many people.

Goblins

They might be small, but gremlins are an especially nasty type of goblin.

Clever, crafty, and mean — that's a goblin for you. Goblins are short, ugly, and cruel creatures found in many fairy tales. Their small, bright eyes gleam out from wrinkled green faces. They have long fingers tipped with sharp claws. Jagged, yellow teeth sneer through their crooked mouths.

There are several types of goblins. Hobgoblins, orcs, and gremlins are just a few. Goblins often enjoy stealing jewelry, breaking dishes, and moving furniture around. If something suddenly breaks or goes missing, goblins are usually to blame.

Legends say that goblins don't like sunlight. They normally sleep in deep caves during the day. Goblins also live in old, dark mines. They love the gold, diamonds, and other shiny treasures they can find in mines. When they find treasure, they usually want it all for themselves. Goblins will often fight to the death over a valuable piece of treasure.

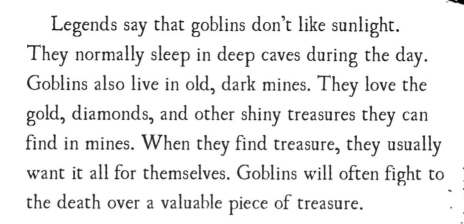

GOBLINS EVERYWHERE

Goblins are popular creatures in many fantasy books, movies, and games. In *The Lord of the Rings* by J.R.R. Tolkien, the heroes fight against thousands of goblins called orcs. In the movie *Gremlins*, hundreds of the wicked creatures terrorize a small town. Goblins are also a popular monster in the role-playing game *Dungeons & Dragons*. The nasty little creatures make it hard for players to succeed in their missions.

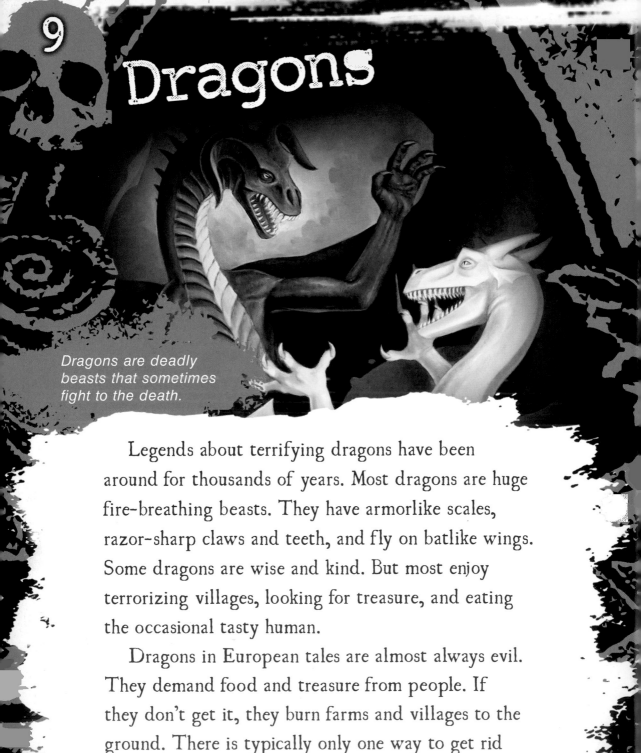

Dragons

Dragons are deadly beasts that sometimes fight to the death.

Legends about terrifying dragons have been around for thousands of years. Most dragons are huge fire-breathing beasts. They have armorlike scales, razor-sharp claws and teeth, and fly on batlike wings. Some dragons are wise and kind. But most enjoy terrorizing villages, looking for treasure, and eating the occasional tasty human.

Dragons in European tales are almost always evil. They demand food and treasure from people. If they don't get it, they burn farms and villages to the ground. There is typically only one way to get rid of a dragon. A fearless knight fights the dragon in combat and finds a way to slay the beast.

REAL-LIFE DRAGONS?

Ancient legends about dragons are found all over the world. Where did the idea of these big, fire-breathing beasts come from? The earth was once home to giant reptiles known as dinosaurs. When the dinosaurs died out, they left their skeletons behind. Dinosaur fossils are found all over the world. It's easy to see how ancient people may have thought the bones came from big dragons. Perhaps this is why stories about dragons are found in so many different cultures.

HORRIBLE FACT

Dragons in Asian legends are usually wise and kind. They often use their magical powers to help poor people. Today, many Asian cultures still respect and celebrate dragons. They are considered a symbol of wealth and good luck.

See it for Yourself!

If you want to see freaky monsters up close, there are several places you can go. At the Haunted Mortuary in New Orleans, Louisiana, you may get a good scare. Inside, visitors can use special equipment to try to track ghosts.

The Mythical Monster Museum in Waxahachie, Texas, is home to hundreds of monsters. People can see statues of vampires, werewolves, goblins, and other creatures of the night. Visitors may even learn a few monster hunting tips they can use at home.

Ugly, hairy monsters are the stuff of nightmares. Long ago, when people saw things they didn't understand, they often thought a monster was responsible. Today we know most monster legends are just stories. But it's still fun to imagine that scary, man-eating monsters might be lurking somewhere in the dark!

Visitors to the Mythical Monster Museum can learn about many legendary monsters.

Glossary

corpse (KORPS) — a dead body

fossil (FAH-suhl) — the remains or traces of plants and animals that are preserved as rock

hoax (HOHKS) — a trick to make people believe something that isn't true

hormone (HOR-mohn) — a chemical made by a gland in the body that affects a person's growth and development

hypertrichosis (hy-per-tri-KOH-sis) — a rare disease that causes thick hair to grow all over a person's body

impale (im-PALE) — to thrust a sharpened stake through a person's body

lair (LAIR) — a place where a creature lives and sleeps

skeptic (SKEP-tik) — a person who questions things that other people believe

Read More

Gee, Joshua. *Encyclopedia Horrifica: The Terrifying Truth! About Vampires, Ghosts, Monsters, and More.* New York: Scholastic, 2007.

Hess, Nina. *A Practical Guide to Monsters.* Renton, Wash.: Mirrorstone, 2007.

Szpirglas, Jeff. *Fear This Book: Your Guide to Fright, Horror, & Things That Go Bump in the Night.* Berkeley, Calif.: Maple Tree Press, 2008.

Internet Sites

FactHound offers a safe, fun way to find educator-approved Internet sites related to this book.

Here's what you do:

1. Visit *www.facthound.com*
2. Choose your grade level.
3. Begin your search.

This book's ID number is 9781429622929.

FactHound will fetch the best sites for you!

Index